CW00675760

Dedicated with love, to everyone

What you are about to read was recorded live from the heart in 2008. I'd like to thank Rene Coffey for capturing that recording and Joanne Jarrett of Totally Typing for transcribing my words. Thanks to Helen Parkins for your very gentle edit of my words to ensure that the spoken speech transferred onto paper without compromising the English language – or my use of it – too much. Thanks, too, to Cally Robson of Invention Intelligence for our powerful coach-to-coach conversations that have helped bring this book to life and to light. I also owe special thanks to two people. The first is my mother for her selflessness, love, and courage. Your struggles have meant that life has always been a comfort to me. The second is Marcus Fellowes: from those singing days to the spiritual pathways, your friendship has helped me along the road to inner success. Finally, a special thanks to all the inspiring clients, colleagues, friends and seminar attendees I have met and worked with, and indeed those that I have not. Remember that life is yours and that you are life.

5

The original audio talk of The Gift of Inner Success is available from www.rasaru.com

"Success is meaningless without

The Gift of Inner Success

Rasheed Ogunlaru

Rasheed Ogunlaru Books

4

Published by Rasheed Ogunlaru,
The Coaching Studio, 223a Mayall Road, London SE24 0PS
Website: www.rasaru.com
Email: Rasheed@rasaru.com
Design by Steve Byrne and Rasheed Ogunlaru

Copyright © Rasheed Ogunlaru 2008

All rights reserved. No part of this publication may be reproduced, stored in a retrieval system, or transmitted in any form or by any means, electronic, mechanical, photocopying or otherwise, without the prior permission of the copyright owner.

fulfillment – both begin within"

Chapter 1

Welcome

Welcome to 'The Gift of Inner Success'.

The Gift of Inner Success was 'revealed' to me 'by chance' during a stage of self discovery during my life journey. The gift is about all the subtle things like acceptance, energy, flow and trust which form the very essence of our existence and which we so often overlook. And it is remembering and embracing this gift that leads to us being well adjusted with ourselves, and in the world, and enables us to live lives of joy, contentment and contribution.

9

There's so much talk in our world about success. But most of that success tends to be externally focused: it tends to be focused on the things that we don't have, that we're looking to acquire. 'The Gift of Inner Success' will help you tap into what you already have. So it's really a kind of spiritual journey, if you like.

For most of us there is a conflict going on between our head – which is telling us to do this, and to do that, and to be this, and to be that – and our heart, which is just authentically wanting us to be ourselves. So if you've ever felt ill at ease, it's probably because there's this conflict between head and heart going on, and 'The Gift of Inner Success' is an invitation for you to go back to a far more centred, still space.

So this book will resonate with you if you're on a personal journey, if you're looking to find self. It will resonate with you if you're on a spiritual journey, and if you're a humanist. You can embrace it if you're religious, and you can embrace it if you're non-religious and believe in people and possibility.

This book will help you to stop, slow down, and re-connect in order for you to move forward and out into the world and be connected in yourself, in your relationships, at work, in business, in your community, and between communities. From there, we can address some of the changes that we want to see in the world.

11

Chapter 2

My Story

It may be useful for me to start off by saying a little bit about myself and my story, but remember, this is very much about you, your story, and where you are.

I was born in London to Nigerian parents, and I had a pretty average upbringing. We certainly weren't well off by any stretch of the imagination. I always felt a little bit like an outsider looking in, and so I've always been able to have a slightly objective perspective on life.

At 18, like many people, I wasn't too sure what I wanted to do, and I ended up working in the media. I had many roles, but one of the things I went on to do was to train people to appear on television and radio. And I remember very early on in my career being asked to do a far more senior job, but I wasn't sure I had the confidence to do it. But then I realised something, and the realisation was this: "Rasheed, you have people skills. If you have people skills, then you can do anything."

These people skills I realised I had were linked to the ability to connect with people, to understand them, to make them feel comfortable, to help them feel at ease with themselves and to then help those people to perform better. So that had a lot to do with what I went on to do in terms of coaching. In fact, back then, I was coaching without even knowing it.

After the first ten years in my job, I was made redundant and I used my redundancy as an opportunity to pursue my real passion – singing and performing. Using my media background, I helped many singers and performers to promote themselves. And then I found something interesting. Many of them struggled with things like 'life-balance', 'confidence', 'money', and 'relationships' – the kind of things that many of us also struggle with, but for these performers everything was amplified because they were in a career that is often perceived to be deeply uncertain. This struck me and, along with a friend of mine – who was an actor/singer and had undergone quite a lot of training – we were both mindful that singers should be connected mind,

14

body, and spirit. Very often, these creative people weren't: instead, they were very dis-connected in mind, body, and spirit.

Together, we formed 'The Mind, Body, and Spirit of Singing', and we helped singers to develop holistically. At this point, my friend handed me a leaflet on life coaching, and we recognised that this might be a good tool to include for helping artists to move forward.

So I went and re-trained as a life coach. During my training, I went on my own inner journey which had, in fact, begun sometime earlier in the lead-up to us establishing 'The Mind, Body, and Spirit of Singing'. As well as developing new skills during the course, something else happened, almost as a reaction to the course, and I found myself writing. I found myself writing on the train, on the tube every morning, and I wrote a book called the 'The Gift of Inner Success'.

With the arrival of the book I realised, over time, that this was the foundation of how I work today. The book – which this incarnation of 'The Gift of Inner Success' distils – explored the subtle things that I touched on earlier in the Introduction that

15

we often overlook. Trust, acceptance, energy, flow. These are the things that are frequently missing in our lives. This realisation had a profound effect on the way that I coach, and I needed to work it and allow it, bit by bit, to just flow into what I was doing. I say 'allow', because I found that this book was speaking a slightly different language from that of lots of other people out there, and my own head was in a quandary as to how to let this simple goal-less knowing, wholeness and acceptance to merge with a system around goals and achievement. But once the heart is in flow, these things take care of themselves. That is what 'The Gift' is all about.

Today I work with people of all backgrounds. I work with people who are asking themselves, 'Where am I going next in my life?' Sometimes they are seeking a career change. Maybe the change has been thrust upon them. Many are thinking about starting or running their own business. Others are singers, performers, and high achievers. I'm increasingly asked to work with young people. I also work within companies. Many of these people, ironically, want to find themselves authentically. But all this, as far as I'm concerned, boils down to the same thing: helping people authentically be themselves – at work, in their relationships, in their business, in every aspect of life. Personal life, relationship life, family life.

Perhaps there's a change that you're seeking. Perhaps you, too, are seeking self.

Sometimes we are on a journey to find ourselves whether we consciously know it or not.

That's enough about my story. What we're going to do is to look at you and where it is that you're at, how you can become centred, and explore in more detail this notion of 'Inner Success'. 17

Chapter 3

The Emperor's New Clothes

18

You know, life is a bit like 'The Emperor's New Clothes'. I don't know if you remember the story from when you were young? I have a colleague – Margaret Parkin – who is a successful author, and who works in training and development. She and her company ('Success Stories') use stories and storytelling to help people to effect change within themselves.

19

Margaret and I were once having a conversation in which she asked me, "Rasheed, what story do you most relate to?" I paused, thought about it, and replied 'The Emperor's New Clothes'. In the story, what happens is that the emperor – who is going to have fancy robes made for an important ceremony – is hoodwinked, and he ends up walking along in his parade, flanked on either side by all his subjects. Of course, the emperor is naked.

The costume of wonderful cloth that has been

woven especially for this occasion is non-existent. Everyone has somehow been mystified: they seem enchanted, they seem to believe that he is in these marvellous robes. From my recollection of the story, it's hard to tell whether all the subjects have been duped in some way, too – or whether they are just too afraid, blind, or bamboozled to see. But then a little boy points out that the emperor is naked, and as soon as he does so, everybody else realises the same thing.

The reason I tell this story is that I feel that we live in a world that's a little bit like that. Deep down, we all know: we all have a sense of wanting to re-connect to ourselves, and yet we're all living in a very externally focused world. We all know that we are living in an illusion, like the emperor, and that there is little or no substance to it. This is why the conflict which I pointed to earlier – between 'head' and 'heart' – happens. It's as though everyone wants to authentically be themselves, but very few people will say it and very few people will speak it.

That leads us to the heart of 'The Gift of Inner Success'. We know a lot about outer success, we know that we're expected to look like this, to be like that, and we're told what we should aspire to personally and professionally. There are all sorts of ideas about who it is you are that you've been told from very early on in your life.

We're also bombarded by messages daily – in the newspapers, on television, on the radio, online, and in conversation with everybody we meet. 'The Gift of Inner Success' invites you to rediscover at what is really at the heart of inner fulfilment, and what is at the heart of true, sustainable success.

So let's begin to look deeply at that. The best way to do this is for you to look directly at your own life.

21

What we're going to begin to do is to look at you – to look at where you are, and to help you to become far more connected in your heart. It may be as you're reading this that you need to 'translate' some of my words into words that resonate with you. I use the word heart; for you, that might be about instinct, intuition, your spirit – whatever it is for you.

Chapter 4

Knowing Nothing

22

Let's start. I'm going to invite you to take a moment to relax. Take a few deep breaths in and out. Take each breath in and out slowly. Perhaps, if you're sitting or lying down, you might want to get a little bit more comfortable. Enjoy this book in whatever way resonates for you. It may be that the words just wash over you, or you might read every word and consider it deeply. It's probably best that you read this with an open mind, and let the words seep in. Let them seep into your 'beingness', so that you're able to enjoy it. This book really is for your heart, although bits of it will be interpreted by your head – and that can be part of the challenge.

23

You're probably reading this because you're at a point in your life where you're wanting to be more authentically yourself. You may be at a point where you're lacking a sense of direction – or that you believe you need it. There may be some changes that have been forced upon you. You may have some concerns or issues about health, about your career, or problems that you're facing in business, or challenges within your relationship. And all these things, whilst they can appear to be very different types of problems and challenges, link to the same thing. They all link to how you relate and respond to your self and your world.

People who seem to be the most well adjusted tend to be those who have a particular kind of a relationship with life, and that's what we're really looking at here.

So what is this 'Gift of Inner Success', this gift of inner happiness?

You know it and you have seen it. You'll know people in your life who seem to have this gift. They may not be rich, although they might be. They may not be very successful in conventional terms. In fact, they may often appear to possess very little in material terms. But they are people who are incredibly centred. They're always smiling – they have warmth. Whatever their personal experience is – and they will all have experienced the same kinds of trials and heartaches that you will have done, sometimes even more – yet somehow they remain balanced, calm, and at peace with themselves and with life. What is it? What is it in their spirit? What is it in their approach that helps them be connected to themselves?

When you distil what most people want in their life, it usually comes down to a couple of things. And these couple of things are what you do absolutely everything that you do for. I remember once I sat down with my best friend who does some work in this area of helping people to become themselves and we sat down and wondered, "What is it that's at the heart of all these things that people wrestle with?" And as we looked at our lives, and looked at everything we knew, and everything that we assumed we knew about life and the world, we came to the realisation that we didn't know anything at all.

We didn't know anything first-hand for ourselves: everything we knew had been learned or assimilated.

So if you were to cast your mind back as early as you can remember, you're not likely to have many thoughts running around your head. You'd be noticing shapes and colours, and you'd have some vague memories. Perhaps as you move forward and advance the years, you'll have pictures in your mind of your mum, your dad, being out in the park, being at home, or running around – or whatever it may be. But all these things, all the names, the labels – "that's a tree", "that's the sky", and so on – all these things will have been labelled for us later on.

So when I sat down with my friend some years ago, and we looked at everything we believed and everything we thought we knew, we realised that, at first, we were simply a blank piece of paper – a blank canvas with huge potential. And that is, of course, what we are as babies. The complicated stuff happens below the level of our conscious awareness. So we breathe naturally. The brain helps to regulate the body and all the complex things in our bodies. If you asked an expert in anatomy, they'd tell you that we are a very complex mechanism. But all these complexities, all the bio-mechanics, we don't have anything to do with. In fact, if you try to think about them, you'll often run into trouble.

For example, if you start thinking about breathing, you'll suddenly start finding yourself short of breath. So the complicated things in life actually go on below the level of our everyday consciousness. On that level, we really know very little about our bodies, the shells within which we exist.

Similarly, when you look externally into the world, most of your ideas – in fact, all of your ideas – will have been picked up bit by bit, stage by stage. So early on, you're told you're a 'boy' or a 'girl', you're 'good', you're 'bad', you're 'bright', you're 'smart', you're not so 'smart', you're 'fat', you're 'thin'. Bit by bit, you are first fed these ideas, and then pick them up. Gradually they become assimilated with other ideas, and thus you develop more complex ideas about the world. And then, later on, you pick up political ideas – other ideas. Over time, you then label these ideas as your own. Over time, you settle with this assimilated idea of who you are and you call it your self.

27

So I sat there with my friend, and we looked at all of this, and we realised that we didn't know anything first hand. Everything had been fed to us and then assimilated. Again, you can look at this for yourself. Do not take 'my' word for it. Do not take in another second-hand idea… take a look for yourself.

Right now, take yourself back as early on as you

can remember, and see if you can notice what it is that you're thinking, what it is you're feeling. The chances are that you won't be thinking much. If there are any ideas or feelings, see if you can go back even further. The chances are that as you do this you'll be feeling much, much lighter because there'll be an absence of content, and this is the space is that we want to be in.

Be mindful that we started off as far more of an empty glass than a full one. But the potential is in there. The potential is there inherent within a baby, just as the potential is there within a seed. This takes us to the root of 'inner success', because, of course, it's the seed, it's the potential. But what happens in life is that things become complicated, and rather than being sat in our hearts, we tend to be caught up in the mind, and the mind, by its nature, is conditioned. So what we need to do is to get back to the heart in order to be centred, in order to be able to make sense of the world, and in order to bring the heart and the head into harmony, and that's precisely what we're going to do.

28

29

Chapter 5

Going Within

We've spent a little time beginning to explore all that you know, all the ideas you have, and how – when you were very young – you didn't have any ideas, and how they came over a period of time. We've begun to explore and experience this space, this stillness that we tend to have at our core. You may have found the silence and stillness refreshing. This is why, very often, you're drawn for a walk in the park, or in another kind of natural environment, and naturally, automatically, you feel reconnected. You're breathing in, you're in balance. You feel at one with yourself and with nature. Your cares, desires and fears are left behind.

Think about what happens if you have an argument, or if you receive some bad news at work or in the family. You probably take yourself off to your room, or go for a walk, or something similar. What you are doing here is going inwards, into yourself. So even when you do an 'external pursuit' like going for a walk, you're actually going back within yourself. You are naturally re-centering yourself, reconnecting to your self. And this is, of course, what we do every night when we go to sleep – we go back within ourselves. Here, as we are asleep –especially outside of the dreaming stages – we have no awareness of our self. We are at one.

So we've begun to explore this space, this stillness, and you may remember that I touched on the two things which tend to be at the heart of what people are looking for.

One of those things that we touched on is peace. We say that we want peace. We want peace of mind, we want peace in our homes, we want peace in the world. We want to learn how to achieve this.

The other thing that we want is happiness: we want to be happy. We want to be happy in ourselves, we want to have a happy relationship, we want to be happy with the work we do.

This is the case for you. You want to be happy in yourself, you want to be happy in your relationships, you want to be happy in your job, in your career, in your business, and with your family. You want your children to be happy, you want your parents or whoever it is that you have in your life to be happy. Your loved ones and friends, your associates: you want those people to be happy.

How can we arrive at this happiness? It's an interesting question, particularly when we live in a world in which we're far more obsessed with success than with happiness. This again points us to 'The Gift of Inner Success', because 'The Gift of Inner Success' is that happiness.

So – what is the root of that happiness, and how can we go back to that root, and how can we then able to achieve meaningful success in everything we do?

Chapter 6

The Story
of Your Life

What I'm going to get you to do now is to take a quick look at your life story. And we're not going to analyse. We're not going to go deep into therapy – there's not going to be a need for that. But I just want you, very briefly, to run through in your mind some of the key events in your life. Do it gently. If there are any painful things, let them go. Just run your mind through the main events of your life.

35

What we're going to do is to look a little at the story of your life.

It may be that you're wrestling with many things in your life that you actually needn't be wrestling with. When I give talks, I often do an exercise in which I'll ask someone in the audience to hand me their bag. If someone's got a handbag or a case, I'll pick it up. You might have a bag near you now. If so, you might want to reach for it. Once the audience member has handed me their bag, I'll rummage around in it. Because in life we're often rummaging around through all the contents of life, trying to sort everything out. We're wrestling with it all – there's papers here, there's cosmetics there, your wallet here, and your pass there. We're constantly rummaging around, trying to sort out all this stuff that was packed in ages ago.

Often there's a lot of stuff in the bag, even though it seems to be quite a small space, and there are various corners in which there are all sorts of things tucked away. This is how we can feel within ourselves. And we often spend hours and hours, years and years even, rummaging around and trying to sort this stuff out.

There's a more powerful and simple way to address your relationship with your life and its contents. Let's just gently take a look at the entire bag and look at all its contents.

You might find that you've got this over here and that over there, and then there's this here... and you'll find that actually all the contents, when we relate this example back to your life, is not your content. Perhaps, for you, there's an issue here

36

about your mother or your father. Or about the absence of them. What's that got to do with you? It was prior to your conscious involvement. There may be issues about your childhood. What have they got to do with you? There may be issues about your characteristics or background. How much of that really has anything to do with you? There may be issues around the things you believe – did you actually choose them? There maybe an issue here about something that did or didn't happen. Again, it may well be prior to your involvement.

Most of the things that we wrestle with are things that are from, or which relate to, very early on in our lives and which we weren't privy to. So as you gently look back over your life, you can find that the content isn't yours. It's a bit like going through your closet, when you're sorting out your clothes and you think, 'where did that come from?', and you discover things that you'd forgotten about, forgotten you had, and hand-me-downs. You'll discover things that are worn out, too big and too small for you, and faded. Similarly, you'll discover things in your life that are now worn out, don't fit, and so on.

So if you are wrestling with who it is you are, it's

37

probably because it doesn't fit with you. Just like if you're wrestling with a jumper that's too tight – if your identity is uncomfortable – then it can't be you. It is not you. Let me say it again: if you're wrestling with something that doesn't fit, then that suggests that it's not truly you. You have outgrown it, or it may never have been right in the first place.

And again, by gently looking at the content of your life, you can begin to let things rest. As you do this you will discover that your identity is simply the clothes you wear. It is not you, and the clothes change with the occasion and the time in life. You are what resides beneath. This is the true self: the self that needs no labels and definition, for it is prior to the labels and definitions.

What we are really looking at here is the story of our lives and letting that false identity to be seen as such. I'll give you two examples of how this realisation became clear to me, because they may help you to look and see through your own.

One of my audio talks is called 'Become Who You Are'. This is really the essence of 'The Gift of Inner Success'. In a way, it expresses the 'Gift of Inner Success' as a means of unravelling your life story.

Soon after I recorded the CD, I was invited to speak at a big personal development show. The show had thousands of attendees and was being addressed by a range of eminent speakers. It was the first time that I'd been asked to speak at such a big event, so I was acutely aware that I needed to perform very well. I wondered what I could I talk about, and I realised that I could really only talk about one thing, and that was about what's at the heart of everything. So I decided to give the 'Become Who You Are' talk. I showed up to give the talk knowing that I couldn't do any preparation for it. I just went out on stage and I talked and spoke from the heart.

39

Afterwards, a young man who was near the front of the audience asked to speak to me. So we arranged for him to visit me at my coaching studio. He wasn't coming to me as a life coaching client as most people do – he just wanted to talk, as the words in my talk had resonated with him in some way.

So we sat down and he told me his life story. From day one, he was estranged from his parents, he was written off very early, he struggled at school, he went off the rails.... Just about all the bad things, the difficult things, the unpleasant things that can happen in someone's life – those things had happened to him.

This young man was about 30 years old. As the story progressed into what happened in his twenties, it was clear he'd become involved in some unpleasant stuff. He didn't tell me the detail, but he didn't need to. And then, as he brought his story up to date, there were two sparks of light in this otherwise quite dark story. One was that he'd met a girlfriend who'd believed in him, and the other was that he'd happened to meet someone who worked in the personal development field who also believed in him. And he told me that he now really wanted to help other people move forward. He wanted to go into schools, and he wanted to work with young people.

When he'd finished – and it took about an hour for him to tell me his story – I asked him a question: "How much of that, how much of the content of your life has got anything to do with you?" He paused and said, "Almost none of it".

His entire life story, all the things he'd wrestled with – starting off from a parental situation that

40

had nothing to do with him, then being written off at school, and getting into trouble – all these things linked to him believing who it is that he'd been told he was. And in that moment he suddenly realised that it didn't have anything to do with him. His life story was a false life story. So the difficulties, those unpleasant things that he'd been involved in – they were unnecessary. They were completely unnecessary and, in that moment, he had that realisation.

It's happened in my life too, this realisation. I was estranged from my father. He'd left home when I was very young. One day, my mother rang me. It was a few days before my thirtieth birthday. Since my mother very rarely calls me, I know when she calls that there's something up, or that I haven't spoken to her in a long time. My mother said, "I've got something to tell you. Your father's died". We were on the phone for a few minutes and then we ended the call.

41

Prior to that moment, prior to that call, I completely hated my father, didn't want to know anything about him, and when he'd tried to get in contact, I hadn't wanted anything to do with him.

At the end of the phone call, suddenly my view

on life changed. There was a moment of realisation. A few moments previously, I'd had all this anger… and then it was replaced by a completely different feeling. I just thought it was very, very sad. This particular person had died, and because of certain decisions he'd made, based on the ideas he had about himself and life, he'd become completely estranged from his family. He'd ended up dying in rather miserable, impoverished circumstances. And all of this – all the things he had done in his life – was due to who and what he believed about himself and how he should be. Again, his story was another 'story', but it had nothing to do with me. All the emotions I had felt earlier in life were based on the story. Once I realised it was just a story, all the emotions fell away in a moment. It just happened naturally.

I'm not saying that we need to be unemotional, or without compassion. In fact, we can actually arrive at true compassion, but first of all we need to realise that our stories are really just that – stories. Our lives are really a series of sensations and events which we label as this and that, good and bad, desirable or undesirable – all based on the labelling and conditioning we have received. That is what life is. The sensations and events can be enjoyable or painful, but they are just that. It is this knowing that is in your heart. This is the birthplace of true contentment.

You can arrive at this right now by looking gently at your own life. You may have had similar examples in which the 'story', the veil of life, falls away and you see life as it is – as the boy did in 'The Emperor's New Clothes'. For instance, you may have experienced moments of ill health, and suddenly life begins to get in perspective. You may have lost somebody, or you may have had a bereavement: suddenly your perspective on that person changes. You lose your job, you're going to be made redundant – suddenly your perspective changes. Suddenly, you realise that the events were just the events. Suddenly, you realise that the person you lost was just a spirit soul trying to find themselves as best they could. Suddenly, you realise you had lost your true identity in the job role you have just lost. Suddenly, you realise that health is a blessing, and life is something to be lived and cherished, not feared. It happens in a moment. There is no process, no analysis. It just becomes clear. Your mind becomes silent and stops spinning stories. You are at one with life. This is 'The Gift of Inner Success'.

All these life events point you back to you, but these things do not need to happen in order for you to become rooted. So what we're going to do in a few minutes' time is to reconnect you to you: to help you let go of the story and then stay centred, and to let this 'Gift of Inner Success' blossom within you.

45

Chapter 7

Embracing Life

We've already covered quite a lot of ground. We've touched on story. We've touched on identity. We've touched on the fact that we seek peace and happiness, and how, by looking at our story, and stepping back from our story and the stories that we've been told about ourselves, suddenly there is space. The space emerges immediately as our mind falls silent and is at peace. And it's this space – this peace of mind – that holds the power.

47

By and large, the people who are most well adjusted have a conscious or an unconscious awareness of this. The pace at which they go in life is often perceived to be slower. They're more still, they hear more deeply, their words are more resonant: they're far better adjusted to themselves and to the world. They have an understanding. One of the quickest ways for you to arrive at this particular point is by looking at your relationship to life. You can either fight life, or your can flow with life. Generally, you'll find that life embraces those who embrace life. It really does come down to that. When you embrace life you are at one with it, and thus you are naturally in flow with it. If you are fighting life, you are at conflict with yourself and thus with everything else, and life becomes fractured, embattled, and a struggle. When you embrace life, you embrace yourself and become at one with all that is. This is what happens, quite literally, when the mind falls silent.

48   It's important that we touch on the theme of conflict. We have conflict within ourselves, in our relationships, and in our world. And the best hope to ease that conflict in yourself, in your relationships at work, and in your community is to be able to arrive at this peace within yourself.

One of the first ways that you can do that is to look at your relationship with life. We tend to live life perceiving things as either 'this' or 'that', and what happens very early on is we're drawn into 'this', or we're told we shouldn't move towards 'this', or to move away from 'that'. Of course, much of this is for our benefit and for our growth. But it actually means that in many practical ways we become stunted. Our lives become lives in which everything is separated, labelled and divided. In the absence of these 'mind-defined' labels there is no conflict.

Prior to the ideas and fears of conditioning there is no conflict. However, as we grow, everything becomes something that is either 'desired' or 'feared'. One becomes seen as many, and this splintering reinforces fear, suffering, misunderstanding and conflict. Even the most everyday things become the stuff of conflict. And so, for example, when you talk about the weather, you might say "Oh goodness, it's such a miserable day." What you're actually saying is that it's raining or it's grey.

49

You are therefore adopting a relationship to life which means that probably about 50% of the time you're going to be deeply unhappy, because you label and therefore relate the rain, the cold, the snow – whatever it is – to misery and disappointment. You can hear this in the language we use every day. The result is that you pine for the sun and recoil from the rain. This is conflict. This is separation.

But this conflict doesn't ever arise for a flower. A flower knows innately that it grows through both sun and rain, not just one or the other. Both are necessary for growth, and both play their part. No doubt in your life it's probably the times that we would label 'dark' or 'difficult' that have led you to the greatest insights, the greatest clarity as to what you were about.

Have you had that experience where, for example, a relationship ends, and you're feeling heartbroken, distraught, devastated, and so upset? And then a couple of years pass, and you realise that actually it was very important: it was necessary for your growth and understanding to move on. Your whole perspective on the relationship has changed and shifted. By having a broader perspective, by realising that life has its sunshine and its rain, and by not fighting, you're in a far more powerful position to be content, to be understanding. It is this that's pointed to by the very word 'understanding'. One must be able to see everything in order to understand, and this is the invitation. You can do this right now simply by embracing life.

I'm going to invite you to spend a moment with wherever you are in your life to go within yourself, to take yourself from your head into your heart area. You might want to take a couple of deep breaths and get more settled.

Whatever your circumstances are, just gently look at them. You may be lucky that things are in a 'good' place, and that you're quite happy about them. Or it may be that there are some challenges that you need to address. Whatever your circumstances, just be in this space of acceptance, of peace, because right now you're changing your relationship to it. Right now, you're just letting things be. Take a little time, let everything be. Right now, don't try to change anything, don't fight anything. Let everything be. Stay in that space a little longer.

51

Of course, we sometimes do this on a very practical level. You'll hear people say that you should sleep on a decision. Sometimes it's just that stillness, that rootedness, which gives us a bit more perspective when we wake up. When we go back within ourselves, we're able to be far more centred and see things for what they are.

This process is 'The Gift of Inner Success'. If we are in a battle with life, we are fragmented from it and ourselves. If we embrace life, we are at one with it and with ourselves. It is as simple as that. We are quite literally part and parcel of life.

Chapter 8

From Head
to Heart

You know that if you were lost in the forest and you'd been running around, the best thing for you to do would be to stop, to be still, and to see where you are, so that you can retrace your steps, retreat to safety or move forward to your destination. Once you stop, you can find your bearings and see the landmarks. You can see the clearings, you can see the dangerous areas, you can see the undergrowth, and suddenly you become alert, you become alive – you become far more enabled. And this is a very natural process, it's 'The Gift of Inner Success'. It's our own innate abilities which, if we don't interfere with them, that we are absolutely at one with, we're absolutely rooted in.

But if we live in the head when 'challenges' happen – when the relationship breaks up, when there are problems at work, when we are fighting with friends, family, or loved ones, when there's an

53

economic downturn, when there are problems out in the world – that's when we get lost.

The invitation is to be still and return to the heart, because when we're at the heart, we're able to understand. It is when we are at our heart that we are quite literally centred. Our centre of gravity is not in our head. When we reside in the head we become off balance, and we sway from one thought, feeling, theory and mindset to another.

When we return to our heart we're able to be at peace with ourselves, we're able to nurture ourselves, we're able to be nourished, we're able to take stock. We are far less ill at ease with ourselves and others, and this is the place where we have the best chance of arriving at peace personally and professionally, and where we are most able to move forward from.

What may be going on for you if there are those challenges in your life is that your heart may be calling to you. It may be telling you, 'You might need to look at this', or 'you need to come back within'. You might be thinking, 'Well, I'm not quite sure about this', or 'I'm not sure where to go', 'there's something that's not right, in this situation'. And this is really is the heart nudging you and calling you, through your mind, to return to your heart – to yourself. It's inviting you to come back home, to yourself. And this is what I describe as 'becoming who it is that you are'. This is all at the root of 'The Gift of Inner Success', and there's nothing that you need to do. It is a natural process of embracing your self.

You may recall how, earlier in this book, I mentioned that the most complex things that happen in life, within ourselves, happen below the level of everyday consciousness. So, right now, your heart's beating, and your blood is being pumped around your body. How does that happen? Unless you work in biology, or are a scientist, you probably don't know the answer. You may have read a few books, but do you really know what's going on? But yet when we're consciously thinking, we think we know everything about the world. We think we know everything about everybody else. In fact, we know very little.

So that day when I sat with my friend and we looked at what we knew, it was liberating for us because we suddenly realised, 'thank goodness for that' – 'I don't know about that', and 'I don't

55

know about that, I just assumed that'. It was the most powerful thing. We'd poured water out of the cup, we became much clearer, and we became much more in balance. The seeing was the freeing.

It may be that you are trying to hold onto too many things. It may be that you're trying to work too many things out. You may be trying to fix an identity which is flawed in itself. Invariably, the identity we have of our self is simply an identity and not the self.

Many people spend a whole lifetime wrestling with an identity that's not theirs. That's why I mention this bag that we've been rummaging around in. But by being still, by being silent, you can be grounded and find a level of 'identity' beneath the level of identity at which you operate. Beneath all the names, all the labels, and beneath all the ideas – it's at the heart of your 'beingness'.

What we're going to look at in a moment is how to foster that silent space within yourself in order for you to be connected. And then you'll become enabled to blossom, because there'll be far less interference, far fewer obstacles. You'll stop seeing life as an obstacle, and from here you'll be best able to tackle the challenges that you face: challenges that you face personally, and challenges that you face wherever you live or work, and so on.

Chapter 9

Peace of Mind

One of the seeds, perhaps the seed at the root of 'inner success', the essence of 'inner success', this 'gift of inner success', is silence and stillness – peace. It's funny how these words will resonate with you. Take, for example, 'peace of mind'. 'Peace of mind' is a phrase that we use often, but do we understand what it means? 'Peace of mind' is a huge clue. You want 'peace of mind'. You want 'peace of mind' personally, financially, and so on. How are you going to arrive at 'peace of mind'? What is 'peace of mind'?

'Peace of mind' is about not being overly drawn into mind, letting your mind be at peace. Being at peace with your mind.

That young man who came to see me and who told me his life story had some very deep and profound challenges. But in answer to one innocent question which intuitively fell from my lips – "How much of

59

that life story had anything to do with you?" – he paused, and there was silence. There was a powerful silence, his mind was silent. His heart answered "Almost none of it", and the story fell away. The false identity that he'd been wrestling with for so many years fell away.

And I said something to him, because he had mentioned that wanted to help people and to particularly work with young people. I said: "Great. That's fine. But with the realisation that you have now, it is enough if you share this in your own life, with your own family". I invited him to foster that stillness, that acceptance – that's enough. In fact, that's plenty, because that will enable them and support them to be able to do the same thing. And I told him that it was also great if he chose to do this work with children. But, I said, you can go into their schools and say to them, "Yes, you can be successful and you can achieve this, this and this," which is fine, and it's noble that you want people to achieve a certain success. But, I continued, there's a difference between that, and you going in and letting them know that you really appreciate who it is that they are now. That you see beyond even the stories.

That you see their hearts – that is powerful, because people know when we've accepted them as they are, at heart. And he knew what I meant.

You may have experienced this in your life: we call it unconditional love, don't we? When someone sees you, they see your heart and we feel still, we well up, we feel very rooted, we feel loved. This is the invitation and this is the only way to 'peace of mind'. The only way to peace in the world is a direct connection.

A prerequisite of peace is understanding, but it doesn't need to be an understanding in a deep, intellectual way. It can be the understanding that we arrive at when we're just being, and when we're just seeing and we're just connecting. You'll see this if you put two babies next to each other in a pen. One parent may have this belief, another parent might have that belief. One baby may be this colour, one may be that colour. But, of course, as babies, they aren't connected on that level. They're just being, beneath the labelling, beneath the stories that haven't been formed yet.

That's what I'm inviting you to look back to. To remember the little boy and the emperor's new clothes. He knew that the emperor was naked and just said it. And suddenly everyone else woke up. All the people in the land woke up and realised that the emperor was naked, and then the emperor felt self-conscious and embarrassed. But the illusion fell away.

Peace is of mind is the end of conflict and separation. It is where the mind falls back into the heart and oneness is known.

63

Chapter 10

Space, Stillness and Silence

64

A friend of mine pointed out that the word 'dis-illusioned' means for the illusion around something to fall away. We tend to think it's a bad thing if you become disillusioned: "Oh, it's sad, they've lost their joy for [something]." But actually it means that the illusion around something falls away, and this is what can happen to you: the illusion around you, the illusion about what's happened in your life – the illusion about it all can disappear.

On this material plane in which we have 'chosen' to live, we come and we go. We live and we die. There is sunshine and there is rain. Something dissolves into nothing and nothing gives rise to something. That is it. It is much like a lava lamp where the shape and form of the lava constantly changes and rearranges. When we embrace these things, life stops being problematic. There will be challenges, but the very nature of those challenges shifts. For example, some people will wrestle for a long time with ill health or an ailment, but there comes a point when they learn to work with that. They focus on what they have, and they flow. Often, they have a deeper understanding of life. This is the invitation to you now, whatever your circumstances. The root to it is stillness and silence.

Stillness and silence seem to be present in many different practices. Many people who are religious will be drawn to silent prayer. Many people will be drawn to meditation. Beyond the realm of those who are spiritual or religious, other people may just take what they call quiet 'me' time. Others go on contemplative walks: they will be contemplating within themselves, they'll be still, and they'll be silent. These are all ways in which we connect to ourselves. This silence is a natural gift. Something happens within them and you know that they just need to be, they need to be aware, they need to be quiet. This is the invitation.

This is the invitation for you now. This is why you were drawn to this book. And if you are silent then information will make itself available to you, but first we must be still. We must be silent. When we are quiet, we can hear. When we are still, we can feel and see. Again, if you're lost in a forest, first of all you stop, and you pause. So it may be that in your life now you're running and rushing around. If you're rushing around in the forest and you're trying to find your way home, this can be very difficult.

But if you just stop and pause, you can look and perhaps remember the path that you took, and that's precisely what we're doing here now. I'm simply inviting you to remember the path you've taken, the path that perhaps you've been led down. The path that you've been encouraged to walk in your life, in yourself, in your identity. But look at it gently, not bitterly.

Those who led you down various paths may have been led down the same path themselves: this tends to be the nature of life. I had that realisation when I mentioned the story about my father. I suddenly realised that it would have been his conditioning – conscious or sub-conscious – and his identity of himself, what he should be or what he shouldn't be, that would have led him to the decisions that he made. And that identity and those ideas would have been first fed to him and so on and so on. What did those 'decisions' have to do with me?

And right now, things that you're wrestling with can dissolve in a moment. The realisation will happen in a moment, and the dust may settle over a period of time. The more it is that you let things be, the more space you allow yourself, the quicker you will be at peace with yourself. But on a practical level, silence and stillness are most likely to be the most profound and powerful routes to being at one with your self. In this stillness and silence, the dust, the debris, the illusion will fall away. But as with any window, dust and debris can quickly collect again, which is why silence and stillness are so valuable.

In a world of noise, in a world of activity, in a world in which everyone seeks 'peace of mind', however much money you may have in the bank – you will not arrive at 'peace of mind'. The one thing that almost everybody has in common is that they lack 'peace of mind'. "Oh, how am I going to do this?", "How am I going to do that?", "What about this?", "What about that?" "How am I going to manage to do this?" "How am I going to manage to do that?" This is the mind. "Oh yeah, but this and this and I've got to do this ….." This is the mind.

68

So stillness, silence, and space are important. Many people know this. This is nothing new: there is nothing ground-breaking here. Many people are saying it in different ways. And stillness, silence and space are ultimately an inner state, even though you may initially re-connect to it through being silent and minimising external noise.

So right now, take a moment whilst you're here to be centred and still. Just embrace life.

In a world of noise, inner silence or the absence of content is the most enriching thing that you can have. And in fact it is a non-doing. We spend so much time doing. But doing is rarely being. Being is seeing. Being is freeing. Being is knowing. Being is sitting within the mystery of oneself. It is the end of questions and the need for answers. It is fulfilment..

69

Chapter 11

Oneness and Compassion

Whatever school of thought or influence you've had in your life, it would seem that there's one root. Of course, that one root might go by all sorts of different names, but it's irrelevant because it's one root. Some will say the root is God, some will say the root is a big bang, and some will say that everything just is.

71

The point is that there's one root. One root, and everyone is inter-related and inter-dependent. But we forget this. We forget that we're inter-dependent. If you could go far enough and look down at the planet, you'd be far enough away not to see the borders and divisions which are man-made, and the divisions which are 'mind-made'. All that really separates us are our thoughts, and we started out without the thoughts. Without names, ideas, and concepts, where are our divisions?

Today, through this book, you've taken yourself

back to the point prior to the thoughts. Those two babies in the pen are not in conflict with each other – they're at peace.

And so by fostering this peace in yourself, there's so much that can blossom, and your innate talents can flow. Then the question arises – what in my life really resonates with me? This is, of course, a question of the mind, and the mind will continue to ask questions. And that is fine because you will know that questions are the nature of the mind. You will know that the mind flutters, but you will be unconcerned by it.

72

The mind will – over time – become more quiet and do the job of working material things out as it does. In that sense, it is the material offshoot of the spirit. They are of one. You're best armed and able to address these questions from this place of peace, and as you gently brush all these thoughts and fears to one side, you'll probably find in your heart that you have particular things that you want to do. Then you can ask yourself: what steps do I need to take in order for that to take place? And there's a plethora of sources of information out there which can help you with that process, but very little that can help you to reconnect to yourself. So I'm not going to spend any time here talking about what you should do and how you should move forward, because the most powerful thing happens when you take that moment to stop.

In fact, as the mind settles back into the heart, you will naturally blossom because you will grow, branch out, and flourish in the direction of the innate and nurtured gifts that you have. It is a natural process. As the fog clears, there is clarity, and one can move forward.

Stop chasing through the forest to become... Instead, gently re-trace your steps. This leads you to where you are and where you have always been. Even the idea of journey is simply that.

What we've done here is to gently re-trace those steps and we've arrived back home through remembering that we already are whole and fulfilled. Any baby would tell you this, if they could – this connectedness, this is joy. This is happiness, this is 'The Gift of Inner Success' and from this gift, everything else can blossom – by being with oneself.

So I'd encourage you to perhaps spend a few

73

minutes after reading this book to be with yourself and to be silent. And if you find it of use you might want to return here from time to time, or to return to whatever works for you and keeps you at peace with yourself. You will find that this inner success pours into all aspects of what you do in all areas of your life.

I wish you every happiness. Take care.

74

75

76

Rasheed Ogunlaru is a leading life coach, motivational speaker and business/corporate coach. His career spans over 16 years in coaching, training, media and performance. His clients include entertainers, entrepreneurs, politicians, professionals, organisations, and the public. He appears regularly in the media on life, work, relationship, business and people issues - including appearances on the BBC and ITV News. He is an inspiring and empowering public speaker and seminar leader - uniquely popular on the business, spiritual and personal development circuits. He is qualified member of the Coaching Academy and is former Co-Director of Samaritans (Central London). He is co-author of A Zest for Business and author of an inspiring range of books, CDs, and MP3s, including The Gift of Inner Success. He has served as the partner business coach of the British Library, running his popular Making it as an Entrepreneur seminar. Prior to his career in coaching Rasheed was a successful communications manager and media trainer, a career which began at 18 when he worked for Which?, the Consumers' Association, and where he became a Press Officer, media trainer and media spokesman. After 10 years he moved on to a career as a singer-performer. On meeting countless performers who struggled with confidence, career progression and happiness, he retrained as a coach to help people take charge of their lives. Today his work spans coaching wealthy high achievers to empowering excluded inner city teenagers. His unique 'become who you are' approach enables people of all backgrounds to achieve greater success, performance, confidence and happiness - from within. As such, he is widely considered one of the leading specialists on achieving lasting inner fulfilment.

For further information on Rasheed's work, or to enjoy other titles, visit his website www.rasaru.com

© Rasheed Ogunlaru 2008

77